dabble lab

ELECTRONICS PROJECTS
FOR BEGINNERS

TAMMY ENZ

raintree

a Capstone company — publishers for children

Raintree is an imprint of Capstone Global Library Limited, a company incorporated
in England and Wales having its registered office at 978-1-4747-5191-9 – Registered
company number: 6695582

www.raintree.co.uk
myorders@raintree.co.uk

ISBN 978 1 4747 5190 2
21 20 19 18 17
10 9 8 7 6 5 3 2 1

• • • • • •

EDITOR
Mari Bolte

DESIGNER
Tracy McCabe

STUDIO PROJECT PRODUCTION
Marcy Morin, Sarah Schuette

PRODUCTION
Katy LaVigne

• • • • • •

Printed and bound in India.
British Library Cataloguing in Publication Data
A full catalogue record for this book is available from the British Library.

Acknowledgements
We would like to thank the following for permission to reproduce photographs:
All photographs by Capstone Studio: Karon Dubke except Shutterstock: elsar, cover
(right), Krasowit, cover (bottom); Illustrations by Dario Brizuela

Design Elements
Shutterstock: TairA

CONTENTS

SPARK YOUR IMAGINATION

Have you ever wondered what makes the blades of a fan spin? Or how a light turns on with the flip of a switch? If you've ever seen the inside of a computer, a phone or an electric toy, you've seen the complex electronics that make these devices work. The wires and circuit boards in these machines transfer electric power to a component. Then the component can perform a certain action. Electronics are essential to making things light up, make noise or move.

5

5

You'll need a few supplies to get started with electronics. You may be able to find some of these items around your house. The others you can get at a hardware or electronics store for just a few pounds.

Materials:
1. solder
2. insulated wire
3. electrical tape
4. cotton balls
5. felt-tip pens
6. brass fastener
7. mini vibrating motor
8. mini LEDs
9. hobby motors with gears
10. 1.5-volt light bulb and base
11. CR2016 or CR2025 watch batteries
12. AAA batteries and battery holder
13. 2 small switches
14. D-cell battery
15. string
16. index card
17. clothes peg with a spring
18. hobby-sized buzzers
19. wooden craft sticks
20. fishing line
21. googly eyes
22. drawing pins
23. disposable plastic cup
24. thick paper
25. cardboard shoebox
26. aluminum wire
27. plastic lid

Tools:
1. glue gun and glue sticks
2. scissors
3. low-watt soldering iron
4. eye protection
5. wire cutting/stripping tool
6. hammer and nails
7. small screwdriver
8. soup bowl and drinking glass
9. pencil
10. large binder clip
11. utility knife

LED NECKLACE

Have you ever seen a necklace that lights up? You are about to make one! This bright and colourful necklace works by completing the simplest circuit. A circuit is a complete path for an electrical current. This project is not only easy to make, it's fun to wear too!

YOU'LL NEED:

CR2016 or CR2025 watch battery
3 LEDs
glue gun and glue sticks
60-centimetre (24-inch) length of string
index card

STEPS:

1: Spread the shorter leads of the LED lights out along the negative side (–) of the battery. (The LEDs should all light up.)

2: Turn the battery so the positive (+) side faces up. Spread the longer leads along this side of the battery.

3: Use the hot glue gun to glue the leads to the battery on this side only.

4: Glue both ends of the string to this side too.

5: Slide the string around your neck to wear it.

6: To switch the necklace off, carefully slide the index card between the battery and the unglued leads.

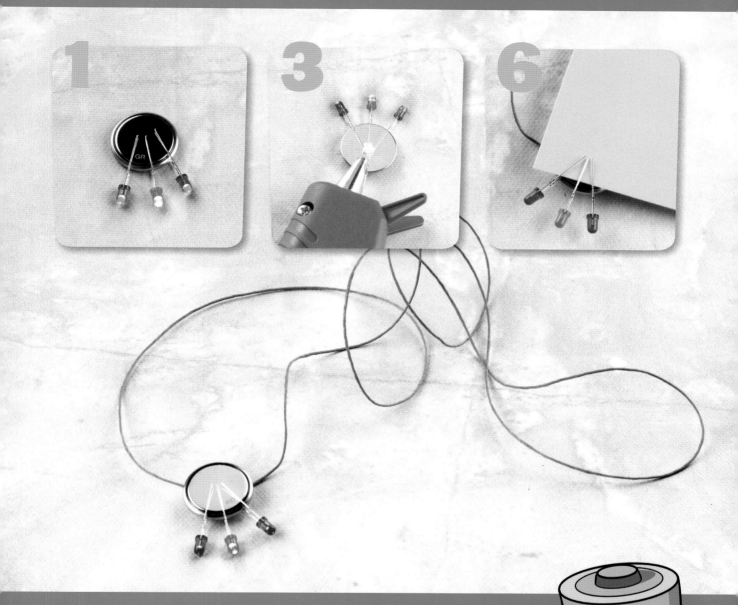

TIP: The longer lead on an LED is positive. It must be connected to the positive (+) battery contact area.

WHY IT WORKS: All batteries have a positive and a negative contact area. They're called terminals. To make a circuit, parts must connect to both the positive and negative areas. This allows power to flow and complete a circuit.

LIGHT-UP
GREETING CARD

Brighten someone's day with this light-up greeting card! This project uses a simple LED circuit with a pressure-sensitive switch. Use your creativity to make a one-of-a-kind card that lights up with the push of a button.

YOU'LL NEED:

12.7-by-30.5-centimetre (5-by-12-inch) piece of thick paper or card
sharp scissors
2 LEDs
electrical tape
CR2016 or CR2025 watch battery
small piece of cotton wool
felt-tip pens

STEPS:

1: Fold the paper in half to make the card. Sketch your designs onto the card so you know which parts should light up.

2: Use the scissors to poke small holes wherever you need a light.

3: Push LEDs through the holes so the lights poke out of the front of the card.

4: Bend the LED leads flat against the paper.

5: Tape the shorter leads to the paper. Make sure you leave about 1 centimetre (0.25 inch) of wire sticking out past the tape.

6: Place the batteries (-) side down on the wires.

7: Place the other leads on the (+) side of the batteries. Tape them to the batteries. The LEDs should light up.

8: Carefully lift the batteries. Tape a tiny piece of cotton under each battery and over each short lead. Now the wire leads should only touch the battery when you press on the cotton.

9: Tape the batteries to the card.

10: Decorate the card, making the lights part of your design. Press the battery to light up your card.

TIP: Tape or glue another piece of paper to the back of the card to hide the batteries.

WHY IT WORKS: A circuit only works when the electronic part is connected to both the positive and negative terminals of a battery. The cotton interrupts this connection until you push it down.

SAFETY FIRST: Ask an adult to help you when using sharp tools like scissors.

MAKE ELECTRONIC CONNECTIONS

Let's take some time now to learn how to make electrical connections. Taping, wrapping and soldering are a few ways to connect wires. Try them out before moving on to the rest of the fun gadgets you'll be making!

YOU'LL NEED:

piece of wood for a work surface
eye protection
insulated wire
wire-stripping tool
electrical tape
brass fastener
low heat soldering iron
solder

TIP: Instructions for the following projects will ask you to connect electronic parts and wires. You can use any of these methods to do it. But make sure you never solder a wire directly to a battery.

SAFETY FIRST: Ask an adult to help you with soldering.

continued

TO MAKE A TAPED CONNECTION:
STEPS:

1: For safety, make sure your work surface is non-conductive. Wood or fibreglass work best. And make sure you protect your eyes!

2: Cut two short pieces of wire with the wire-stripping tool.

3: Use the wire-stripping tool to remove about 2.5 centimetres (1 inch) of plastic from one end of each wire.

4: Twist these ends together.

5: Tightly wrap the wires with electrical tape.

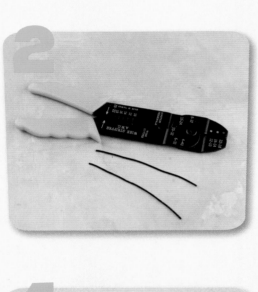

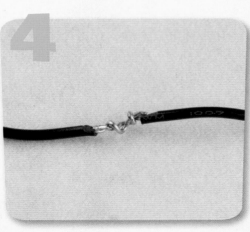

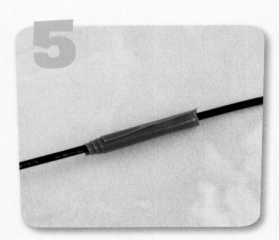

TO MAKE A WRAPPED CONNECTION:
STEPS:

1: Cut two short pieces of wire with the wire-stripping tool.

2: Use the wire-stripping tool to remove about 2.5 centimetres (1 inch) of plastic from one end of each wire.

3: One at a time, wrap these ends around the brass fastener right under its head.

4: Open the legs of the fastener to hold the wires together.

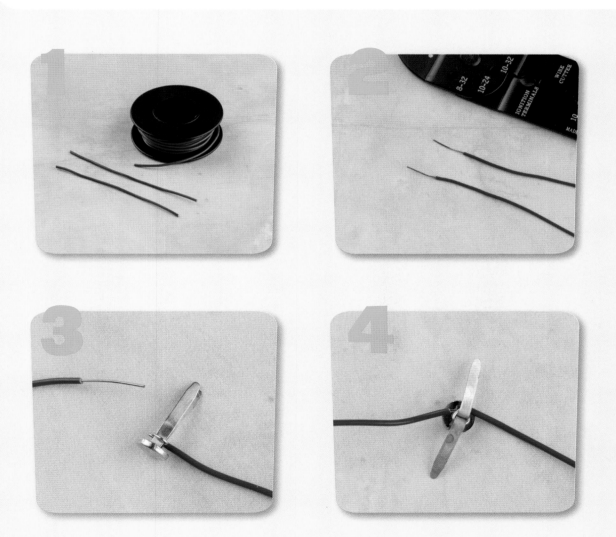

continued

TO MAKE A SOLDERED CONNECTION:
STEPS:

1: Wear eye protection when making a soldered connection. Cut two short pieces of wire with the wire-stripping tool.

2: Use the wire-stripping tool to remove about 2.5 centimetres (1 inch) of plastic from one end of each wire.

3: Twist the ends of these wires together.

4: Lay the twisted wires on the wood.

5: With an adult's help, hold the hot soldering iron tip on the twisted wires.

6: Hold a piece of soldering wire near, but not touching, the tip.

7: When the wires heat up, the solder will flow onto the wires and connect them.

8: Quickly remove the soldering iron tip as the solder begins to flow.

9: Blow on the connection to cool it. Be careful not to touch it until it cools.

TIP: Never touch the tip of the soldering iron or hot solder!

WHY IT WORKS: Soldering is the best way to make connections. You'll need to learn to solder to make more advanced electronics. But twisting and taping is a good way to test out your connections to make sure they work first.

MAKE A SIMPLE CIRCUIT WITH A SWITCH

The most basic electronic system is a simple circuit. A simple circuit transfers power from a source, such as a battery, to an electronic device like a light bulb or motor. Wiring a switch into your circuit allows you to turn the flow of power on and off.

YOU'LL NEED:

scissors

two or three 12.7-centimetre (5-inch)-long insulated wires with 2.5 centimetres (1 inch) stripped at each end

AAA battery holder

small switch

small vibrating motor

AAA battery

STEPS:

1: Twist a wire around each of the metal loops on the ends of the battery holder.

2: If your switch has wires already attached, twist one 12.7-centimetre wire to one of them. If it does not have wires attached, twist one of the 12.7-centimetre wires around one of the switch's metal loops. Then connect the switch to the battery holder.

3: If your switch has wires already attached, skip this step. If your switch does not have wires attached, twist one end of the third wire to the other loop on the switch.

4: Connect the two free ends of the switch and battery holder wires to the ends of the motor's wires.

5: Place the battery in the holder.

6: Turn the switch on to start the motor.

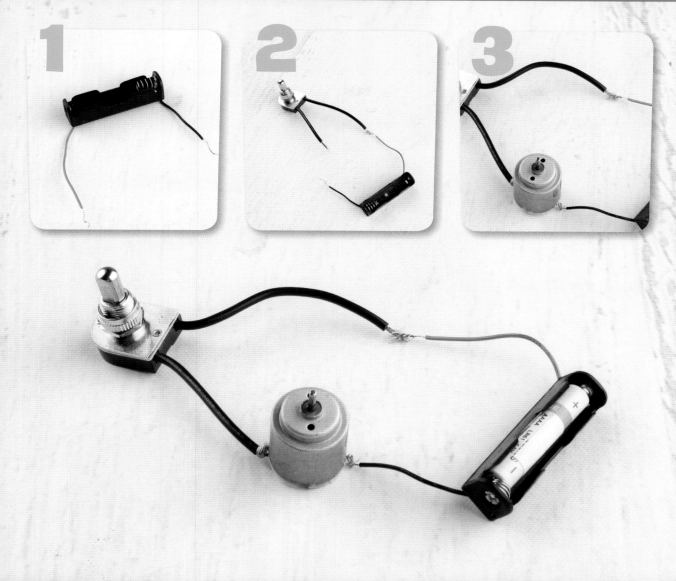

1

2

3

TIP: You can solder the wires in steps 1-4 if you want. This will ensure a good, solid connection. When soldering to plastic parts, make sure you keep the soldering iron tip away from the plastic. The hot tip will melt plastic.

WHY IT WORKS: The switch interrupts the flow of power through the circuit. You can also make a circuit without a switch. To turn off the power, just disconnect one of the wires.

TRIP WIRE BUZZER

Want to catch your brother or sister sneaking into your room? A buzzer is a simple electronic component that you can hook up in a circuit. The switch is activated by a trip wire and will set off the buzzer, alerting you that there's an intruder!

YOU'LL NEED:

clothes peg with a spring

two 20.3-centimetre (8-inch)-long insulated wires with 5 centimetres (2 inches) stripped from each end

glue stick and glue gun

hobby-sized buzzer

electrical tape

CR2016 or CR2025 watch battery

wooden craft stick

1.2 metre (4 foot) length of fishing line

2 adhesive-back hooks

STEPS:

1: Open the clothes peg. Wrap one end of a wire around one of the clothes peg's tips.

2: Wrap one end of the second wire around the other tip. When you close the clothes peg, the bare ends of the two wrapped wires should touch.

3: Glue each of the wrapped wires onto the outside of the clothes peg.

4: Connect the other end of the wire from step 1 to one of the buzzer leads.

5: Tape the other end of the second wire to one side of the battery.

6: Tape the remaining buzzer lead to the other side of the battery. The buzzer should begin buzzing.

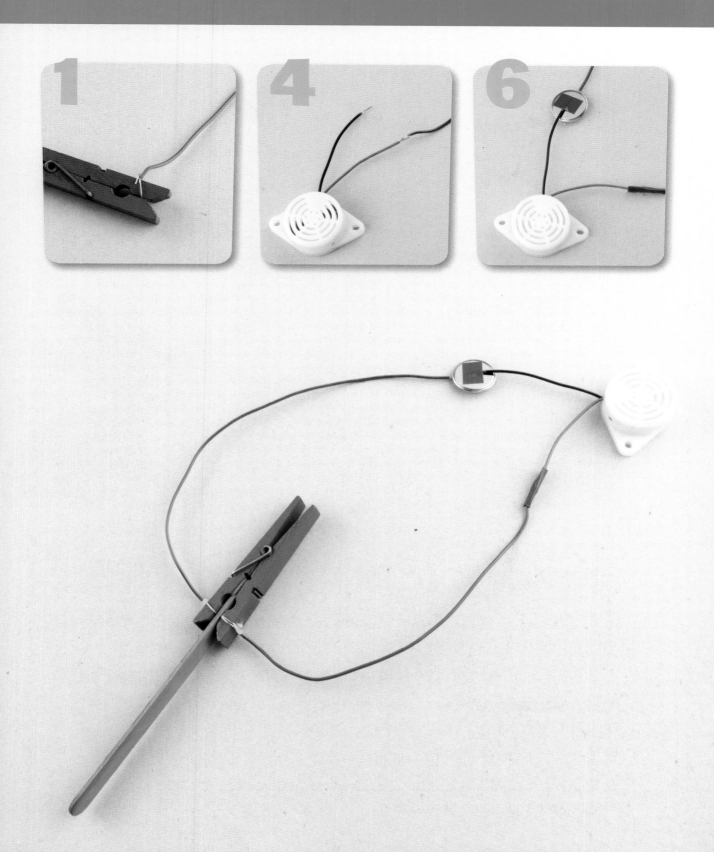

7: Insert one end of the craft stick into the clothes peg to interrupt the circuit. The buzzer will stop.

8: Wrap one end of the fishing line around the other end of the craft stick. Glue it in place.

9: Stick the hook onto the edge of a door frame. It should be about 7.6 centimetres (3 inches) from the floor.

10: Stick the other hook to the other side of the door at the same height.

11: Stretch the fishing line across the doorway. Tie it to the hook from step 10.

12: Now wait. When someone walks through the door and trips on the fishing wire, the buzzer will sound.

TIP: If you want, you can hook up an LED or small light bulb instead of a buzzer.

WHY IT WORKS: Anything that interrupts a circuit acts like a switch. In this project, the craft stick works like a switch.

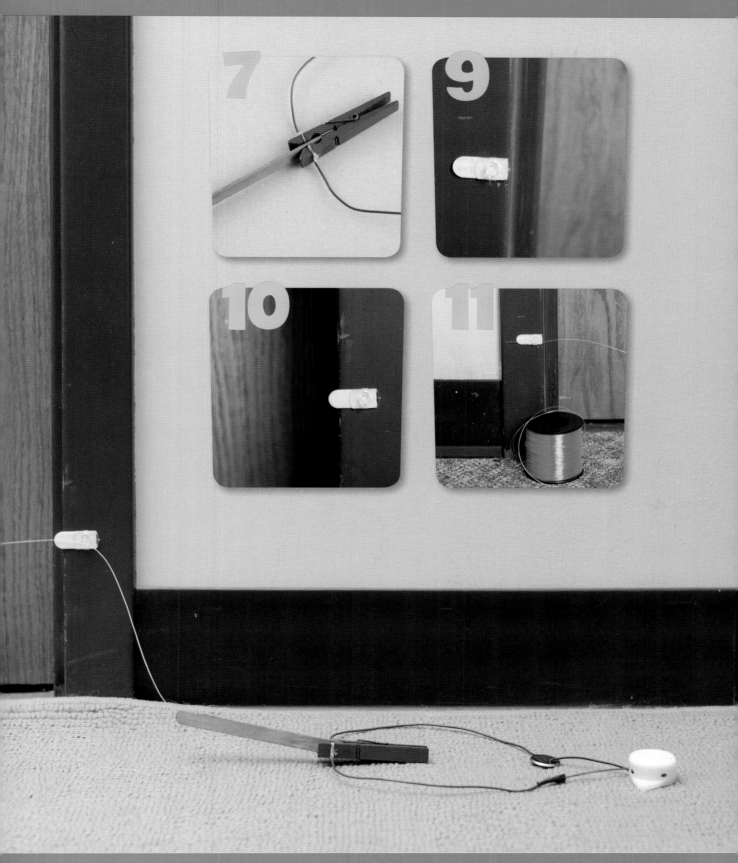

MINI TORCH

Torches are a common household item. But did you ever think you'd be making your own? Let's put your skills to the test while building this mini torch.

YOU'LL NEED:

1.5-volt light bulb

1.5-volt socket base

three 10-centimetre (4-inch)-long insulated wires with 2.5 cm (1 inch) stripped from each end

small screwdriver

electrical tape

D-cell battery

mini switch

thick paper

soup bowl and drinking glass for tracing

pencil

scissors

STEPS:

1: Screw the light bulb into the base.

2: Wrap wire tightly around each of the screws in the base.

3: Use the screwdriver to tighten the screws.

4: Tape one end of one of these wires to the (+) end of the battery.

5: Place the base on the (+) end of the battery and tightly tape it down.

continued

6: Tape one end of the third wire to the bottom (-) end of the battery.

7: Connect each of the unattached wire ends to one of the loops on the switch.

8: Tape the switch to the side of the battery. Flip the switch to turn on the light bulb.

9: Turn the bowl and cup upside down. Trace them on the paper to make a donut shape.

10: Cut out the donut. Slit it in one place and shape it into a cone. Tape the base of the cone around the top of the battery.

TIP: The positive (+) side of the battery is the end with the raised bump.

WHY IT WORKS: Your torch has all the same parts as a torch you would buy in a shop. However, when your battery stops working, you'll have to remove all the tape to replace it!

MINI FAN

This mini fan will be perfect to keep you cool on a hot summer day. A hobby motor may be small, but its power will blow you away!

YOU'LL NEED:

AAA battery

large binder clip

three 7.6 centimetre (3 inch) insulated wires with 2.5 centimetres (1 inch) stripped from each end

hobby motor with gear

electrical tape

mini switch

2 wooden craft sticks

glue stick and glue gun

STEPS:

1: Slide the battery inside the binder clip. Fold the clip's legs back.

2: Connect a wire to each of the motor leads.

3: Tape the motor's side to one of the clip's legs. Make sure the shaft and gear are angled upwards, away from the binder.

4: Tape one of the motor wires to one end of the battery.

5: Connect the other motor wire to one of the switch tabs.

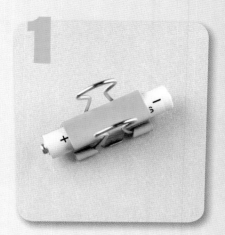

continued

6: Connect the remaining wire to the other switch tab. Tape the switch to the side of the motor.

7: Tape the end of this wire to the other battery end.

8: Glue the middle of a craft stick to the middle of the gear.

9: Glue the middle of the other stick to the first one. The two sticks should form an X.

10: Flip the switch to start the fan.

TIP: Before attaching, soak the craft sticks in warm water overnight. Then twist them to look like angled fan blades. Let them dry. The angled blades will give your fan even more cooling power.

WHY IT WORKS: Much like an aeroplane's wings, the shape of a fan's blades directs air in different ways for maximum flow.

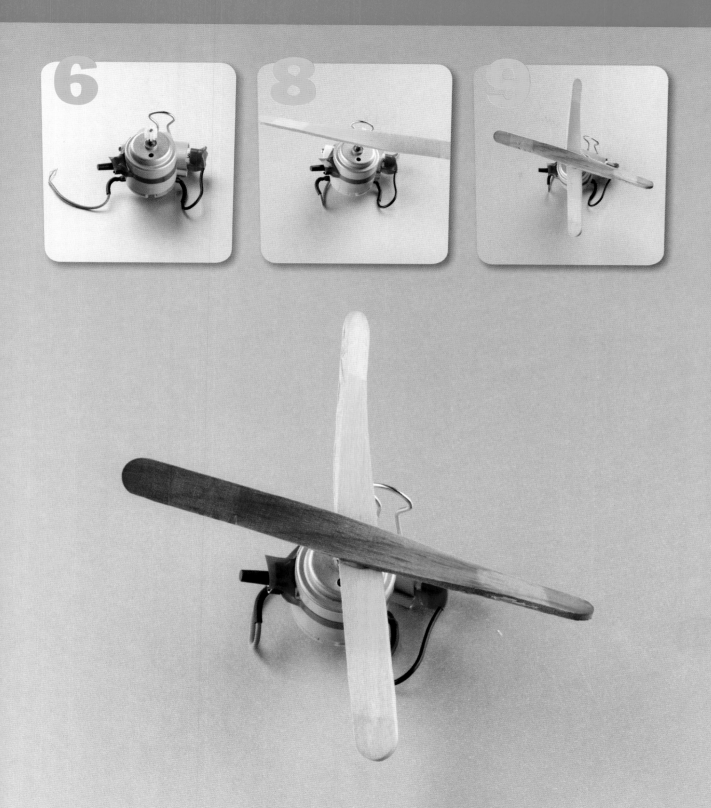

BUZZER GAME

If you like games, then this project is for you! To win, you must trace a kinked wire without touching it. If you're not careful, you'll set off the buzzer and lose the game.

YOU'LL NEED:

cardboard box about the size of a shoe box

sharp scissors

46-centimetre (18-inch)-long aluminum wire

electrical tape

hobby buzzer

CR2016 or CR2025 watch battery

two 15-centimetre (6-inch)-long insulated wires with
2.5 centimetres (1-inch) stripped from each end

STEPS:

1: Turn the box upside down. Poke two small holes on opposite sides of the box bottom with the scissors.

2: Poke about 2.5 centimetre of each end of the aluminum wire through each hole.

3: Turn the box over and bend each end of the wire over. Tape the ends to the inside of the box.

4: Turn the box over. Shape the aluminum wire into a number of kinks and bends.

5: Tape one buzzer lead to one side of the battery.

SAFETY FIRST: Ask an adult to help you when using sharp tools.

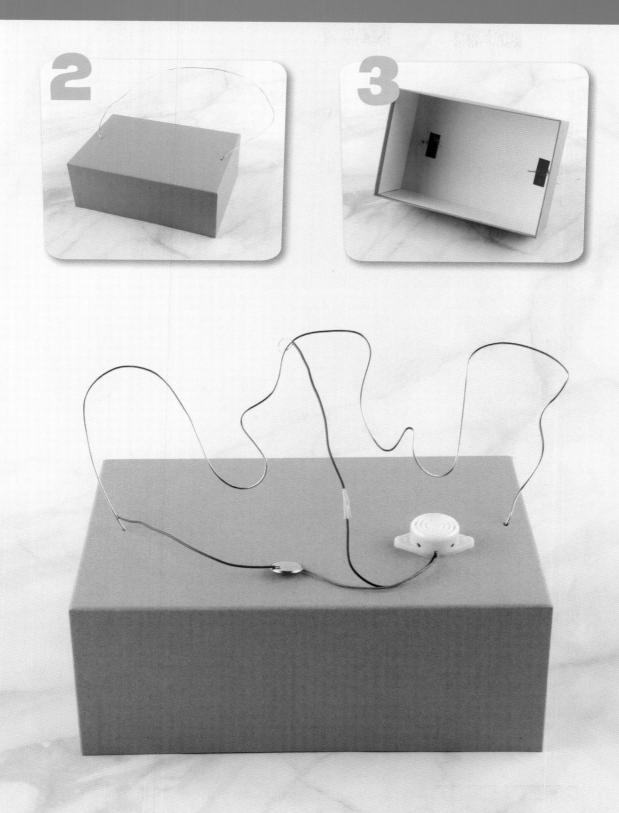

6: Tape one end of an insulated wire to the other side of the battery.

7: Connect the other end of this wire to the aluminum wire near one of its ends.

8: Connect one end of the other insulated wire to the remaining buzzer lead.

9: Loop the other end of this wire around the aluminum wire. (Make the loop slightly larger than the aluminum wire.)

10: Starting on one end of the aluminum wire, trace it with the loop. Trace the loop as quickly as you can to the other end without setting off the buzzer.

TIP: The more bends and kinks in the aluminum wire, the more challenging the game will be!

WHY IT WORKS: When you touch the loop to the aluminum wire, you complete the circuit. To stop the buzzer sounding, you must not let the wires touch.

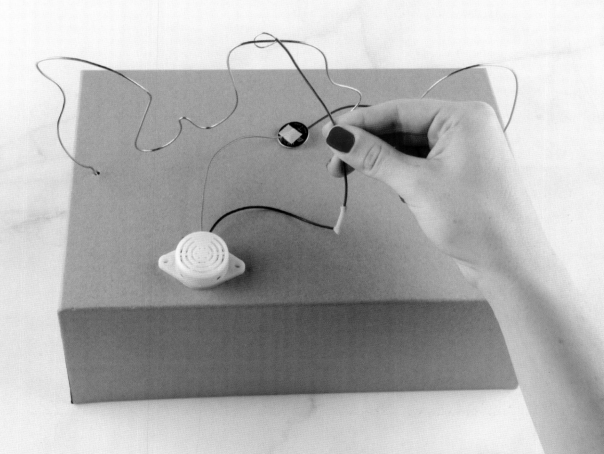

LADYBIRD ROBOT

Robots are fascinating machines that can do everything from cleaning a floor to assembling a car. For this project, you'll be making your very own robot! A tiny vibrating motor will have this bug bot buzzing all around.

YOU'LL NEED:

black permanent marker

plastic lid from a jar, about 5 centimetres (2 inches) in diameter

glue gun and glue sticks

large googly eyes

pencil

card

scissors

small vibrating motor

AAA battery holder

electrical tape

3 plastic drawing pins

AAA battery

STEPS:

1: Use the marker to decorate the lid. Make it look like a ladybird.

2: Glue on the eyes.

3: Trace the lid onto the card. Cut out this circle.

continued

4: Connect the motor wires to each end of the battery holder.

5: Tape the motor and battery holder to the middle of the card circle.

6: Push the drawing pins into the other side of the circle. Space them evenly around the edge. Then put the cardboard circle down, using the heads of the pins like legs.

7: Insert the battery into the holder. The circle should start moving.

8: Gently place the lid on top.

9: Remove the battery to stop the bug bot.

TIP: If your ladybird stops moving, try adjusting the battery and motor.

WHY IT WORKS: The vibrating motor causes the pins to shake and move. The vibrations slide the ladybird across a flat surface.

5

6

7

CRAZY ART BOT

There's no end to the fun you'll have watching this art bot. It uses a hobby motor to spin across a sheet of paper and create an amazing piece of art.

YOU'LL NEED:

utility knife

disposable plastic cup

two 25-centimetre (10-inch)-long insulated wires with 2.5 centimetres (1-inch) stripped from each end

hobby motor and gear

AAA battery holder

AAA battery

electrical tape

felt-tip pen

2 large googly eyes

glue gun and glue sticks

large sheet of paper

STEPS:

1: Ask an adult to cut a 6-centimetre (2.5-inch) hole through the centre of the bottom of the cup.

2: Connect a wire to each of the metal tables on the motor.

3: Connect the gear to the motor shaft.

SAFETY FIRST: Ask an adult to help you when using sharp tools like a utility knife.

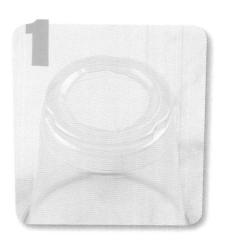

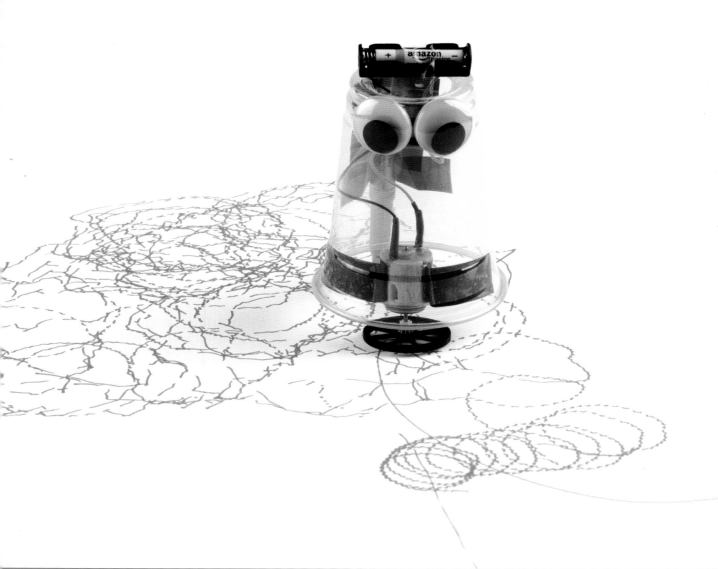

continued

4: Tape the motor to the inside wall of the cup. Make sure the gear sticks out about half a centimetre (¼ inch) above the top of the cup.

5: Thread the wires through the opening on the bottom of the cup.

6: Attach each of the wires to one of the wire loops on the battery holder.

7: Tape the pen to the outside wall of the cup. Make sure it is directly across from the motor. Adjust the pen so when its cap is removed, its tip is even with the gear.

8: Glue the eyes to the outside of the cup above the motor.

9: Place a battery in the battery holder to start the motor.

10: Remove the pen's cap. Then place the art bot, gear side down, on the paper.

11: Watch it create!

TIP: Add a switch to the circuit to turn off the art bot. Otherwise, remove the battery to shut it off.

TIP: You may have to adjust the motor or pen to balance the art bot.

WHY IT WORKS: A motor shaft spins around causing things, such as wheels, to turn. In this case, the spinning motor causes the cup to spin around.

GLOSSARY

circuit complete path of an electrical current

current flow of electrons through an object

insulated covered with a material that stops heat escaping

LED light-emitting diode; LEDs give off visible light when an electric current passes through them

non-conductive unable to conduct heat or electricity or sound

solder low-melting blended metal used for joining two metal surfaces

switch part of a circuit that turns electrical objects on or off

terminal positive and negative contact area of a battery

volt unit for measuring electricity

watt unit for measuring electrical power

FIND OUT MORE

BOOKS

Electrical Engineering: Learn It, Try It! (Science Builders), Tammy Enz (Raintree, 2017)

Experiments with Electricity (Read and Experiment), Isabel Thomas (Raintree, 2015)

From Falling Water to Electric Car: An Energy Journey Through the World of Electricity (Energy Journeys), Matthew Manning (Raintree, 2015)

WEBSITES

www.bbc.co.uk/education/clips/z7k3cdm
Ideas for using simple circuits to make games and activities.

www.tate.org.uk/kids/make/art-technology/make-drawing-robot
A step-by-step guide to creating a drawing robot.

INDEX